Wedding Etiquette 101

The Essential Etiquette Guide To Wedding Planning, Budgeting, Invitation, Rehearsal, Ceremony, And More

Denise L. Witt
Copyright© 2014 by Denise L. Witt

Wedding Etiquette 101

Copyright© 2014 Denise L. Witt

All Rights Reserved.
Warning: The unauthorized reproduction or distribution of this copyrighted work is illegal. No part of this book may be scanned, uploaded or distributed via internet or other means, electronic or print without the author's permission. Criminal copyright infringement without monetary gain is investigated by the FBI and is punishable by up to 5 years in federal prison and a fine of $250,000. (http://www.fbi.gov/ipr/). Please purchase only authorized electronic or print editions and do not participate in or encourage the electronic piracy of copyrighted material.

Publisher: Enlightened Publishing

ISBN-13: 978-1499387735

ISBN-10: 1499387733

Disclaimer

The Publisher has strived to be as accurate and complete as possible in the creation of this book. While all attempts have been made to verify information provided in this publication, the Publisher assumes no responsibility for errors, omissions, or contrary interpretation of the subject matter herein. Any perceived slights of specific persons, peoples, or organizations are unintentional.

This book is not intended for use as a source of legal, business, accounting or financial advice. All readers are advised to seek services of competent professionals in the legal, business, accounting, and finance fields.

Table of Contents

Introduction 3

Chapter 1: Etiquette for Financial Responsibilities 5

    Bride's Family 8

    Bride Herself 10

    Groom's Family 11

    Groom Himself 12

    Other Financial Responsibilities 13

Chapter 2: Invitation Etiquette 15

    Invitation Wording 16

    Addressing Invitations 19

    Children 21

    Refreshments and/or Reception 23

    Additional Activities 24

    Private Invites 25

    Maps 26

    Wedding Website 26

Chapter 3: Wedding Gift Etiquette................ 29
   Thank You Note Gift Etiquette.................. 33
   Wedding Cancellation 35

Chapter 4: Rehearsal & Reception Dinner Etiquette.. 37
   Rehearsal Dinner 37
   Reception 41

Chapter 5: Wedding Attire Etiquette 53
   Bride and Groom Ensemble Etiquette....... 55
   Attendant Attire Etiquette 59

Chapter 6: Ceremony Etiquette....................... 73
   Religious Differences 73
   Vows.. 77
   Walking Down the Aisle 80
   Attendant Choices...................................... 81

Chapter 7: Wedding Exit Etiquette................ 87
   Bouquet Toss... 87
   Change of Formal Clothing 88
   Send Off 88
   Getaway Car.. 90

Conclusion 99

Introduction

Nothing can steal pleasure and create hard feelings or bad memories about your special day than accidental wedding etiquette faux pas. For most people, a wedding is one of the most important and memorable days of their entire life. And while some complications and situations cannot be foreseen, planned for, or avoided, there are many problematic areas of wedding etiquette that you can solve or prevent if you just have the information needed to do so.

This guide is intended to lay out some aspects of wedding etiquette that are the most important to handle correctly both for your own sake and for the sake of your loved ones who will be involved. The more etiquette mistakes you can avoid, the more everyone will enjoy celebrating the launch of your marriage with you.

Now, let's get started!

Chapter 1: Etiquette for Financial Responsibilities

The financial responsibilities that come with a wedding are often a great source of tension for *anyone* closely connected to the wedding – not just the bride and groom. But while the potential for financial drama is high, the risk and severity of problems between those involved is greatly limited simply through respecting the current etiquette guidelines that are common today.

Modern-day wedding budgets plans have changed significantly just in the last couple of decades. The changes in financial etiquette guidelines might be unfamiliar or even unacceptable by older generations in both families.

If there are those who do not agree with modern financial etiquette, it is important for you to "choose your battles" and determine which things are worth the stress and conflict to argue about, and which areas or people are too stressful to negotiate with. If possible, it is most helpful to have a face-to-face meeting between you and both sides of the families in order to have a budget that all parties are in agreement with from the very beginning.

It is becoming more popular for the bride and groom to be responsible for the costs incurred with your own wedding which seems only fair – especially if you want a lavish wedding. You may prefer to pay for most or all of the wedding expenses yourselves in order to create the wedding you have envisioned without burdening your parents with the cost of various 'luxuries" or having to get expenses "approved" by those paying for them.

The cultural trend of the "older" bride and groom having established careers before marriage is another reason why more of the wedding expenses are being paid for by the older bride and groom who are able to afford the expenditures. Having most of the financial responsibilities on your shoulders can actually be a learning tool that would help you learn how to communicate better as well as chance to learn money management as a couple strengthening your marriage before you are even married!

Another issue that can further complicate traditional wedding etiquette rules is the high rate of parental divorce. The problems that can be present in many areas of wedding preparations if either of your parents is divorced can be challenging even in the best of scenarios with the additional considerations needed for stepparents.

Current guidelines for wedding financial etiquette are below, but they are no longer "set in stone" as they were for previous generations. The guidelines are somewhat flexible if need be in order to accommodate the transition from etiquette of the past when meshing with current and complicated situations.

Another interesting trend in wedding finances is dividing the total wedding expense by three – one part each paid for by the bride's family, the groom's family, and the bride and groom together, each paying a third of the costs. If all parties are amicable with little potential for dramatic conflicts, dividing the costs by three seems to be the most logical and reasonable solution. But in situations where conflict already exists or is expected once money becomes involved, it might be easier to follow traditional guidelines in order to limit as much stress as possible.

While there are a few gray areas in current traditional wedding etiquette in terms of financial responsibility, in general, wedding etiquette breaks down the expenses into five different categories: the bride's family, the bride herself, the groom's family, the groom himself, and the bridal attendants.

Bride's Family

- Planning expenses – this would include the fees for services of a wedding consultant, a wedding planner, and/or the cost of books, computer software, or do-it-yourself instructional material.

- Bride's attire – Including the wedding dress, shoes, jewelry, hair & makeup (also acceptable for the bride to pay).

- Floral arrangements – including ceremony, reception, and other miscellaneous flowers (might also pay for bridesmaids' bouquets as a packaged florist deal).

- Wedding day transportation – to wedding and reception locations.

- Photographer

- Videographer

- Travel and lodging expenses for the wedding officiant if coming from out-of-town location

- Lodging for bridesmaids – this is optional and only necessary if offered to them when asked to be a member of the wedding party

- Reception expenses – traditional etiquette dictates the reception costs be paid for by the bride's parents who are then given the honorary roles of host and hostess tasked with the additional responsibility of making sure the wedding guests feel welcomed at the reception. These expenses include catering, cake, and decorations.

- Grandmother's corsages (sometimes paid for by groom's family)

- Printing and stationary needs – invitations, ceremony program, reception napkins, thank you cards, etc.

- Church fees

- Musical fees – soloists, choir, special music, etc.

- Possibly responsible for bridesmaids' dresses if specific designer, color, and/or style required

- Responsible for their own attire on the wedding day

Bride Herself

- Attendant flowers – bridesmaids, flower girls, etc. (sometimes bride's parents will pay for bridesmaids' bouquets)

- Bridesmaids' gifts

- Groom's ring and present

- Wedding attire and accessories (if not paid for by bride's parents)

- Bridesmaids' luncheon

Groom's Family

- Rehearsal dinner – can be small and limited to the wedding party only, or a big party including wedding guests, but never bigger than the wedding reception or appearing to be in competition with the reception quality

- May pay for alcohol for the wedding reception in order to offset the financial burden

- May pay for part or all of the floral bill also to aid in lessening financial responsibilities

- Corsages and boutonnieres for immediate family of one or both parties

- Lodging for the groomsmen –an optional expenditure and only necessary if offered to them when asked to be a member of the wedding party

- Family wedding attire

Groom Himself

- Marriage license
- Officiant's fees & and pre-marital counseling fees
- His wedding attire
- Bride's bouquet
- Mother's and grandmother's corsages if not paid for by the bride and groom's parents
- Engagement and wedding rings
- Bride's wedding gift
- Groomsmen's gifts
- Groomsmen's boutonnieres, gloves, ties, etc.
- Transportation for the bride and groom at the end of the wedding
- Honeymoon
- Wedding gifts for both sets of parents

Other Financial Responsibilities

- Best man – arrange and pay for bachelor party

- Bridesmaids – arrange and pay for bachelorette party

- Junior Attendants – wedding attire paid for by their own families

- Attendants – Bridesmaids and Groomsmen: their own wedding attire, gifts for the bride and groom, and transportation to and from wedding location.

When looking at the financial aspects involved with a wedding, it is important to remember the wedding is just the first day of the rest of your life as one. Finances are a challenging part of life for most people in the current state of the economy and money is tight for everyone so financial responsibilities of a wedding can cause the great conflicts. Everyone involved should remember the true goal of a wedding is to celebrate the start of another family and be focused on their future together without obsessing over the details.

As financial arrangements are ironed out, "don't sweat the small stuff"! Everyone needs to be willing to compromise with expenses because getting along in the future is more important than any financial expenditures involved with the wedding itself. Above all, etiquette regarding finances should emphasize love and respect first and foremost without expecting those paying wedding expenses to do so at the cost of their own financial well-being with luxuries that are unnecessary for you to begin a happy life together.

Chapter 2: Invitation Etiquette

Using proper etiquette with your wedding invitations is one of the most valuable tools you have while preparing for your wedding – especially in terms of "drama" avoidance. Conversely, failing to follow invitation etiquette can open the door for multiple conflicts from the start.

The invitations may seem like a small part of the whole picture in planning your wedding, and in perfect families, the invitations *would* play a small role. But most families are far from perfect and the invitations can do a lot to soothe hurt feelings help you begin to establish autonomy from your parents.

Invitations are also a source of information for the recipients in terms of family dynamics – especially if there have been divorces or other complications with the parents on either side. How the invitation is worded will explain which parents are or are not involved with the wedding celebration which can be quite helpful to know with divorce and surrounding issues.

Enclosing information on various details along with the invitation is helpful in cutting down the stress load of answering all sorts of various wedding topics that friends and family will ask, and enclosures will also provide the information necessary to make it possible for those invited to share in your joy in the least complicated ways possible.

Proper invitation etiquette guidelines can include such things as the wording, attendance of children, meals & refreshments, additional activity invitations, private wedding/reception issues, maps, wedding websites, attire suggestions, hotel & travel, reply card, at home cards, etc.

Invitation Wording

The wording you choose to invite loved ones to your wedding might take some careful consideration depending on the circumstances. Wording etiquette guidelines should be followed as closely as possible in order to prevent some hurt feelings that might come up while also making sure those who are paying for the wedding are given the proper respect. This is also a place to honor parents that are no longer living if that is desired.

- The most common wording is used when the bride's parents are paying for the wedding which calls for their names first in "requesting the honor of your presence", etc.

- If the groom's family is paying then their names would come first, otherwise it is optional whether to include the names of the groom's parents after the name of the groom.

- If both sets of parents are sharing in the wedding costs, the names of the bride's parents are first then joined by "and" the names of the groom's parents before "request the honor of your presence".

- If both sets of parents are sharing the costs equally with the bride and groom as well, the invitation begins with your names followed by "together with their parents", "request the honor…"

- If you are paying for the wedding yourselves, the wording would then include only your names requesting the "honor of your presence".

- The wording gets a bit more complicated when the bride's parents have been divorced but are still paying for the wedding. Usually, the name of the bride's mother (along with her husband if applicable) comes first followed by "and" the name of the bride's father (and his wife).

- When either of your parents are deceased and you want to honor them in the invitation, it is perfectly appropriate to do so as long as the wording is not ambiguous or inferring the parent is still alive and personally sending the invitation. It is best to include a deceased parent in the same way they would be mentioned in the invitation if still living only with the addition of the word "late" in front of that parent's name.

Addressing Invitations

The etiquette of addressing the outside envelopes for wedding invitations can seem complicated but it is relatively simple to do so correctly in most situations if you know the proper etiquette guidelines.

- Addressing wedding invitations should be done using handwriting – not pre-printed labels of any sort. The wedding invitation sets the official tone for your wedding and shows your style and level of care which are less than your best if pre-printed labels are used.

- Always spell out degrees or titles that your guests may have such as Doctor, Reverend, etc. and place before their names. Do not use initials at the end of the surname such as Dr., Rev., etc.

- Always use "Mr. and Mrs." when addressing for a married couple. If the couple is not married but living together, or if they are married but do not share a last name, address the invitation to both of them – one name per line in alphabetical order.

- Send separate invitations to each person of a dating couple if they are unmarried and do not live together.

- Etiquette for any guests in the military or retired from the military with a rank similar to or above lieutenant or captain should be spelled out next to their names with the specific branch of the military listed below the name. If the guest is retired military, follow the same protocol only add (Ret.) after their last name on the invitation address. If the military guest is below the rank of captain or similar, their title is not written out in front of their names, but the branch of the military service they belong to should be written out below their names in every case of active or reserved officers, noncommissioned officers, and all enlisted military members.

- When sending an invitation to a family with children, you do not need to write the names of the children on the outer envelope. It should just be addressed to the parents while the names of children invited should be written out on the inner envelope of the invitation. If you do not write out the specific names of the children on the inner envelope it is implying the children are not invited so be careful to address properly to indicate your preferences.

- The inner envelope should be addressed to "Mr. and Mrs." with their last name only along with the names of the children if they are invited. If the invitation is being sent to close friends and family, you can address the inner envelope with the common name there are known by in your relationship such as "Aunt Patty", "Mama Cille", etc.

- If the invitation is going to a single person but you also want to let them know they are welcome to come with someone else, address the inner envelope to that person then add "and Guest".

Children

You may or may not wish for the children of your guests to be invited to the wedding and/or the reception, and it is polite to indicate that preference in the wedding invitation. It is easiest and least offensive to take care of supplying this necessary information in the invitation envelope to hopefully avoid the situations you wish to avoid.

One way to make your preference clear is to either include or not include the names of the children when handwriting the inside envelope of the invitation that is used to clarify exactly who is invited within that household. It is also acceptable to include an additional handwritten note inside the invitation to explain your preferences such as: "While we enjoy children greatly, this wedding (and/or reception) is an adult-only event".

You may also mention that only children who are a part of the wedding party or members of immediate family will attend. You can also state your wishes that children are welcome at the ceremony itself, but the due to space or cost limitations, the reception is for invited adults only.

If you are aware of specific situations that might be more problematic on your day, it is perfectly appropriate (for either yourself or other close family members) to contact those guests directly to make sure your preferences are understood and complied with.

Refreshments and/or Reception

It is best to inform your wedding guests through the invitation as to if or what will be available for refreshments or reception in order for them to plan accordingly.

- **Cake & Punch, Etc.** – If you are not having a formal reception or your reception is for privately invited guests only, it is appropriate to add wording immediately following the printed reception location on the invitation that "Cake & Punch will be served in the great hall following the exchange of the vows", or "Light refreshments will be served following the ceremony", etc.

- **Reception Dinner** – If there is a sit-down dinner following the wedding ceremony, there are usually at least 2 entrées available for the invited wedding guests to choose from. While some caterer's do not request those choices until the waiter asks the guests while seating at the reception, some caterers require advance notice as so the count for each entrée option. If that is the case, the RSVP or Reply Card enclosed with the wedding invitation can also mention the choices available with the request to indicate choice when returning the reply card, but nothing about the entrée choices should be on the invitation itself.

Additional Activities

Current trends in wedding celebrations often include several different celebratory activities before or after the wedding itself that require separate invitation and RSVP responses. The activities might include a big family picnic or cookout the day before the wedding, or perhaps a casual brunch the day after the wedding or anything else you wish to do for a more memorable and prolonged celebration.

It is best to include a separate invitation/RSVP card inside the wedding invitation envelope in order to inform the guests of the invite, but the RSVP cards can be simplified to include all the different wedding activities that you need a head count or response with. The wedding invitations you send to people that are only invited for the wedding itself should not have the additional RSVP cards as that is considered to be very rude and offensive if they are not invited.

Private Invites

Another popular trend seen more often in today's society is the preference for a very small and exclusive wedding ceremony followed by a celebratory reception that is often designed to feel more like a fun party than the average wedding reception.

If a private exchange of the vows is preferred, wedding invitations can be diplomatically worded while still making sure your wishes will be recognized and honored. Etiquette protocol for this situation suggests that the invitational wording be altered from "…request the honor of your presence at the wedding reception of …". That should make it clear enough that the ceremony itself is very private, but it is also wise to make that decision early on in the wedding plans in order for the word to get around about how your wedding is being arranged.

When the ceremony itself is by private invitation only, those few who are to be a part of the private ceremony can receive a simple but separate ceremony card inside the wedding reception invitation itself in order to give them the details they need to attend a private ceremony.

Maps

Miniature maps to the wedding location have been a common component of wedding invitations for many years. That is a little less common in this age of GPS and smart phone applications that can be used to make it to the wedding locale, but including unique little maps in your invitations can be a charming personalization. Maps are most useful if the wedding location is different from your hometown, or if you have out-of-town guests coming.

Wedding Website

A more recent addition to wedding planning and invitations is the wedding website that many couples develop when planning their wedding and the rest of their life together. It is a centralized location that loved ones are able to access in order to find any information they might need, and also a central location for you to care for the myriad of details involved with planning weddings, honeymoons, and setting up the new household.

This is also a great place for gift registries, etc. While it is inappropriate to refer to anything gift-related with the invitation, it is appropriate to include the URL address for your wedding website to the invitation. If including this address, you would place it in the lower left hand corner of the invitation or it can be printed on business-type cards and enclosed with the invitation.

You may decide to take care of everything necessary in terms of wedding invitations and guests on this website leaving the mailed invitation to be as simple as possible with few or no enclosures. It can be used for RSVP purposes, maps, and times of the various activities, hotel information, etc.

Chapter 3: Wedding Gift Etiquette

The etiquette surrounding the whole issue of wedding gifts is one of the most important aspects of wedding planning to be aware of and handle appropriately. Faux pas in this area can portray an image which may be nothing like who you are as a couple, and can cause you to come across as greedy, shallow, and self-centered.

Gifts are one of the most enjoyable aspects of a wedding for both you and your guests when etiquette guidelines are employed. But conversely, making poor choices on this matter or ignoring proper etiquette when planning your wedding can rob your guests of the level of pleasure they could find in celebrating your marriage and being a part of your future in whatever meaningful ways are chosen that can be enjoyed by recipients and gift-givers alike.

Here are some of the frequently notorious etiquette aspects of wedding gifts known to be confusing and/or offensive.

- It is NEVER acceptable to ask for a wedding gift and there are no exceptions for this rule if proper etiquette guidelines are followed. It is also considered inappropriate to request specific gifts or money, and wedding registry information should never be included with any invitations or wedding communications sent through the mail.

- Invitation etiquette dictates no inclusion of gift registry or information of any kind that refers to gifts. If you are using a personal wedding website to organize and publish your wedding details, it is appropriate to include a link to your wedding website in the invitation, but nothing specifically for gift requests or registries.

- Gift Registries – Wedding etiquette states the only acceptable way for sharing gift registry information is through word-of-mouth when guests request that information from anyone in the wedding party or family and friends. The only place appropriate for any kind of official gift registry information is if you are using a wedding website. In that scenario, it is appropriate to have links to any wedding gift registry you are a part of on the wedding site itself, but only links to the website of the registry. There should be no specific gift requests on the website either.

- Gift Table – In some regions or cultures, having a gift table set up at the wedding ceremony or reception location is acceptable in order for guests to leave gifts for you. Etiquette for this situation suggests that one or two trusted people within the wedding party be responsible for these gifts which are usually not opened until you return from the honeymoon.

- Cash – Requesting cash for gifts, having a cash tree, or having a money dance during the wedding or reception is considered very poor etiquette – especially when following traditional wedding guidelines. This rule has been ignored more frequently in today's culture but most people still consider it to be in poor taste whether following "old" etiquette guidelines or newly evolved ones. In fact, this a situation is most condemned by wedding guests whether publically mentioned or not so it is highly inadvisable to allow anything that even hints of greed for cash in a something that will be a life-long memory – your wedding. However, there is an appropriate way to have cash be part of your gift registry. There are websites and financial institutions that allow wedding registry for specific savings accounts meant for the honeymoon, home purchase, etc. The protocol to follow for cash gift registries is no different than the other gift registries in that they should not be specifically mentioned anywhere officially except for a link of the wedding website or when asked in person.

Thank You Note Gift Etiquette

- For gifts received at a wedding shower, thank you notes should be sent within 2-3 weeks following the shower.

- Early wedding gifts may be opened and thank you notes sent before the wedding (but gifts are not to be used until after the wedding ceremony has been completed).

- All wedding gift thank you notes should be mailed within 3 months following the wedding. If you find yourself behind in your thank you note writing, consider calling those who mailed gifts to assure them you did receive the gift, and then send a written thank you note as soon as possible.

- Thank you notes need to describe the gift that was sent along with some explanation of how you are going to use it in your new life together.

- If the same person gives you different gifts for different occasions such as an engagement party, bridal shower, wedding ceremony, etc., separate thank you notes should be sent for each separate occasion a gift was given.

- Using decorative or informal thank you notes is acceptable etiquette for engagement and shower gifts, but formal white or ivory thank you notes should be used for wedding gifts. If you are using embossed stationary with your name and/or initials, keep in mind that pre-wedding gifts acknowledged before the wedding must use your maiden name. Married names or monogrammed stationary should not be used until after the actual wedding.

- It is both appropriate and practical for you both to share in the task of handwriting thank you notes after the wedding.

- Pre-printed thank you notes are never acceptable…notes must be handwritten and personalized according to the gift and the giver.

- The notes need to be neatly written without crossed out words or ink smudges, etc. No pencils or colored pens should be used – blue or black ink only.

- Money gift thank you notes don't need to state the amounts given, but how you will be spending or saving it should be expressed along with the appreciation.

- It is a thoughtful and appreciated (but not required) personal touch to send a picture of you together from wedding photos but only if the photographer can supply quickly without needing to postpone mailing thank you notes because you are waiting on the photographer.

Wedding Cancellation

If the wedding gets cancelled for any reason, proper etiquette dictates that wedding gifts be returned post haste. This is why wedding gifts are not to be used until after the wedding. They may be opened and thank-you notes sent before the wedding, but nothing is supposed to be used until you are officially married.

Chapter 4: Rehearsal & Reception Dinner Etiquette

Any time food is involved with various ceremonies throughout your life, there are appropriate etiquette guidelines to respect while enjoying the most common part of celebrations – the food. There are two main areas that food etiquette knowledge is needed in terms of wedding protocol – the rehearsal dinner and the reception (cake & punch refreshments and/or full sit-down dinner).

Rehearsal Dinner

In some ways, the rehearsal dinner may be even more enjoyable than the actual wedding reception because it is supposed to be an informal, relaxed occasion with only you, the wedding party and close family and friends in attendance. There are usually no traditions that need to be accomplished with the rehearsal other then it being a time to connect privately with loved ones and enjoy the future life together that you will be embarking on the next day.

Although not required, a few things can be accomplished during this time in order to make it more memorable while also caring for details that should be covered sometime throughout the wedding plans and ceremony.

- The "rehearsal dinner" most often happens the evening before the wedding directly following the rehearsal of the wedding ceremony by all of those involved with the wedding party. While it is traditionally stated as "dinner", this is not a hard and fast rule as to its timing. The rehearsal can be held any time of the day so the meal following it could be a brunch, a luncheon, early dinner, etc. The main detail is the meal is held after the "work" of the rehearsal is done and enjoyed mainly by just those involved in the rehearsal. It is also appropriate to invite close family members on either side that have traveled from out-of-town to celebrate with you.

- Traditionally, the groom's family is responsible for the rehearsal dinner including the planning, hosting, and the costs associated, but tradition has slowly loosened the etiquette rules involved. Modern etiquette allows the bride's family to care for it if necessary or preferred, and it is acceptable for both families to take care of the planning, costs, and hosting details together. Arranging the rehearsal dinner can also be a great place to allow your families a chance to collaborate and get to know each other whether the groom's family is in charge or not.

- If the groom's family is responsible, etiquette dictates the bride's family needs to provide some specific details to the groom's family as soon as possible in order to give them the information needed to plan accordingly. The groom's family needs to know:

    1. when and where the rehearsal is being held.

2. the style of the reception that will be held after the wedding (how big, how elaborate, which colors, etc.). This is mainly to make sure there is no hint of "upstaging" the reception dinner by the rehearsal dinner which is very inappropriate wedding etiquette. Regardless of finances available, the rehearsal dinner should never be more elaborate or flashy than the wedding reception.

3. names and mailing addresses for those who need to be invited to the rehearsal dinner. As the groom's family may not know everyone involved in the wedding party or close family, indicating why each guest is invited would be a polite gesture, but not required.

- This dinner is meant for the purpose of the two families joining in a relaxed atmosphere to enjoy either beginning or continuing to develop the bonds that will be shared once you are married and officially begin your lives together. This is the time for toasts and funny stories that are not mean-spirited, but allow everyone to get to know aspects of your upbringing and personalities.

- You may or may not speak or make toasts yourselves, but this is the best time to acknowledge each other's parents showing the respect you will continue to give them. It can also be a time for you to acknowledge other family & close friends in attendance with appreciation for their roles in your life in the past as well as the future.

- The rehearsal dinner is also the most appropriate place for the maid of honor and the best man to give their gifts to you. Conversely, you can also give your attendants gifts during this time accompanied with verbal appreciation that might be hard to include anytime during the wedding day itself.

Reception

The etiquette guidelines for the wedding reception are very important to both know and follow, especially if you prefer to avoid offending any of your wedding guests. While some etiquette protocol for receptions is intense and inflexible, the timing of your wedding reception can give some appropriate space to personalize your reception for your own needs and preferences.

The etiquette to follow differs greatly depending on whether your reception is to directly following the wedding ceremony itself, or if it is to be held a few hours after the ceremony is over.

- If your reception is held immediately following the wedding ceremony, you cannot invite guests to only the wedding itself and not the reception or vice-versa. When the reception is back-to-back with the ceremony, wedding invitations automatically infer invitation to the reception and if you desire to follow appropriate wedding etiquette, there are no exceptions to this rule. It is rude and offensive to ask or expect some wedding guests to leave while others are enjoying the reception dinner.

- However, it is perfectly acceptable to start your wedding reception after some time has passed following the wedding – usually a couple of hours. If that is what you have chosen to do, etiquette calls for two separate guest lists – one for those who are only invited to the wedding ceremony itself, and a separate guest list for those invited to both the ceremony and reception dinner. The wedding invitations you mail out also need to carefully include or not include reception details. Extra care is needed to make sure the wrong information is not included depending on reception preferences.

- It works well for most weddings to have a gap of time between the ceremony conclusion and the start of the reception. Not only does it allow guests not invited to the reception a chance to disperse with dignity, it also allows guests who are invited to the reception a chance to freshen up while allowing you a chance to finish wedding pictures and/or rest for a little while in order to gain a "second wind" of sorts to fully enjoy the celebration of your nuptials.

- If unable to afford a traditional full sit-down-dinner at your reception without cutting down your guest list in inappropriate ways, consider less expensive options such as cake & punch receptions, buffet-style receptions, light refreshment receptions, etc. It is more appropriate to cut costs by the type of reception you have than to cut down the guest list of those that should be invited if following proper etiquette. In terms of wedding etiquette, it has become quite appropriate to hold wedding ceremonies earlier in the day which can be very beneficial to the costs of a reception as holding a reception at dinnertime is always more expensive than a wedding breakfast, brunch, or luncheon. There are appropriate and enjoyable methods allowing for a wedding reception with any budget constraints that will follow etiquette protocols while still saving money.

- It is very important to communicate the reception style with the guests via the wedding invitation in order for them to plan their day accordingly. For example, if you are only having a cake & punch reception, your guests need to know that beforehand so they can eat a meal before attending the wedding if necessary or preferred. If children are included in the invitation it becomes even more important for the parents to know in advance in order to avoid conflicts caused by hungry, cranky children. An example of giving the information to your guests in their wedding invitations could be including something along the lines of "Please help us celebrate by enjoying cake & punch with us in the fellowship hall of the church immediately following the ceremony".

Reception Cuisine

Sometimes the foods chosen for a reception need to be carefully discussed between both families in order to respect different cultures and traditions as much as possible. If you come from different religions or cultures, there may be aspects of the food offered during the reception that would make it very uncomfortable for some of the guests. As you want to make sure all your guests are able to enjoy the reception as much as possible, compromises between cultures and religions should be explored and agreed upon long before the wedding day.

Entrée Options

While you most certainly do not need to take into account everyone's particular tastes and preferences concerning food choices for your reception dinner, it is best to have 2-3 different options available that would meet as many different needs as possible.

For example, if you want to offer a pork centered entrée, you might need to consider making sure the other entrée is a meat acceptable for those who have religious convictions against eating pork. If there are a significant number of guests expected who follow a vegetarian life-style, consider having a vegetarian entrée as one of the food choices.

You will never be able to meet everyone's dietary preferences unless you set up a short-order cook for your reception and even then there are dietary restrictions that can't be met by a short-order chef on site. The point is to carefully consider what 2-3 options you are offering for your sit-down-dinner and choose those that would meet the needs of the majority of your guests.

In essence, proper etiquette calls for your reception menu to include parts of the cuisine that will provide adequate nourishment to 99% of your guests whether or not they eat the entire meal selected.

Alcohol

Having alcohol at your reception is a highly individualized choice for many reasons including cost, drinking preferences, guest safety following the reception, enjoyment, etc. Your own individual preferences and the preferences of both families should be considered when deciding whether to offer alcohol at your wedding reception.

However, one etiquette guideline concerning alcohol is always clear – it is never appropriate to have a cash bar or expect your wedding guests to pay for their own alcohol consumption at the reception. Even if you want to allow alcohol consumption at your reception, if you cannot afford to supply the alcohol yourself, then it should not be offered. Etiquette guidelines consider it better to simply offer tea, coffee, soda, juice, water, etc. than to make alcohol available only to those who can pay for it.

Seating Arrangements

There are some specifics to follow when considering the seating arrangements for the guests at your reception and it is very important to follow the appropriate etiquette in these situations in order to make sure your guests are treated as respectfully as they should be.

- Children invited to the reception should have group seating according to age, not social preferences or according to "importance".

- Reception seating should also reflect family gatherings in similarity to family reunions and should never be arranged according to marital status whether married or single. Single guests should be seated within their own families and not at tables set aside for "singles".

- As with anything else involving humanity, reception seating will never be "perfect" or without silly conflicts popping up because of the seating arrangements. Inevitably, the only people who might possibly be totally content with their seating assignment are those who are seated at the table of honor with you or other wedding party members. Even that may not be "perfect" for some so don't even attempt to achieve the perception of perfect seating for your wedding guests as it simply won't happen.

Reception Timing

Tardy arrivals are a problem of any wedding reception or other gatherings for that matter. A couple of solutions that may lessen the frustrating impact of trying to resolve the complications of those arriving late to the reception include using a "fake time" or adding a catchy phrase to the invitation in order to gain guest compliance with the perfectly appropriate reception etiquette you desire – timely arrival. How or if you use these tactics depends on your own unique set of friends, family, and circumstances.

Some groups will find all that is necessary in order to request appropriate manners of being on time is a simple emphasis within the invitation such as "We would love to appreciate your prompt arrival at the reception", etc. This can also be a fun place to show a little of your own style and personality in the wording that communicates your request for guests to follow wedding etiquette rules by being on time.

If your circle of friends and family are known for their tardiness (or if you are!), the time for the wedding reception that is printed on the invitation could be a "fake" time stating the reception will begin an hour earlier than it is truly set to begin. It is debatable whether it is appropriate or not to use this tactic as it penalizes those who are polite enough to be on time for special occasions they are invited to. But if you anticipate significant delays and frustrations stemming from late arrivals, it may be worth considering.

First Toast

The first toast given at the reception dinner should be offered by whoever is hosting (and paying) for the reception. Generally the parents of the groom are tasked with the first toast which should be a welcoming toast to the guests attending the wedding.

Etiquette guidelines suggest the bride's father should return that toast officially starting the first round of toasts that can be offered by anyone who feels so inclined. If the father of the groom is uncomfortable with offering the first toast, it is appropriate for any member of the groom's family to do so instead.

Reception Music

Depending on the type of music chosen for the wedding reception, the decibel level of the music may be a consideration needing your attention. A guest should never take the position of requesting music levels to be lowered which makes it all the more important for you to be conscious of the noise level of the music in order to attend to the needs of your guests. It works best if you or the host set parameters before the reception requesting music be kept at whatever levels preferred.

Normal etiquette guidelines for this are set so the music becomes progressively louder as the party carries on late into the night in order for it not to be too loud for older guests who usually begin leaving a party earlier in the evening before the younger set gets more enthusiastic in their party behaviors. This also allows for a wilder side of partying you might want to enjoy before heading off on your honeymoon.

No Business

Another etiquette faux pas for any wedding reception is the inclusion of business advertisement for anyone including yourselves. There should be no business networking, sales pitches, advertisement flyers, or business arrangements made during a wedding reception. If necessary, scheduling such discussions for a later date is acceptable but should be arranged quickly then dropped as a topic of conversation.

Chapter 5: Wedding Attire Etiquette

Clothing choices and faux pas avoidance are rarely more important than the day of a wedding. There are plenty of ways to express your own unique style within your wedding while still following etiquette guidelines and perhaps asking your guests to follow certain etiquette boundaries and/or style preferences as well.

Unlike some of the other aspects of weddings etiquette, wedding apparel for the bride and groom is still quite similar to the etiquette guidelines of the past. Even brides who rarely wear dresses in normal day-to-day and life occasions find wearing a wedding dress to be personally significant to their fantasy wedding day.

The majority of weddings today still hold a healthy respect for some of the traditions of the past while also acknowledging current fashion trends. For some brides, the wedding attire involved for the bride, groom, and attendants is one of the most important details of wedding planning and usually has been a topic of daydreaming and fantasy since childhood. Whether the wedding dress you choose for yourselves, or the requested attire for your attendants, wedding finery is a display of your own unique tastes and fashion sense.

Certain protocols need to be respected in order to not only be the beautiful bride and groom you want to be on the day of your wedding, but etiquette choices will also help make sure you can look back at your wedding day through photos and videos without regretting the overall style your wedding exhibited.

Etiquette guidelines for wedding attire are based on what time of day the vows will be exchanged, where your wedding is being held, and how formal you want the wedding to be.

- **Time** – In terms of definition, a "daytime" wedding is one that occurs before 6 pm while an "evening" wedding is one that begins after 6 pm or even right before 6 pm with the celebration continuing to much later evening hours.

- **Formality** – While the time of a wedding is easy to define, the definition of "formal" is much looser defined. Formality includes the overall picture you want your wedding to portray and not just a single detail of the wedding here and there. The formality of the wedding walks hand in hand with the style of the wedding.

Bride and Groom Ensemble Etiquette

Formal Bride Attire

Formal weddings can be held during the day or the evening either one and a long, white dress is always appropriate for the bride to wear when the wedding is formal. Even though strapless gowns in general are considered to be formal wear, wedding etiquette prefers strapless bridal gowns used for a formal, evening wedding, but that is an etiquette guideline that is somewhat flexible according to taste and wedding time.

Formal Groom Attire

The groom just might be the easiest to dress for a wedding as a tuxedo will be appropriate for almost every wedding scenario and style. Current fashion trends in tuxedos are perfectly acceptable, but a wedding might be a rare chance for the groom to wear spectacular attire commonly used in days gone by such as a morning suit complete with waistcoat and/or cummerbund, old-fashioned ascots and ties, etc.

A wedding is an opportunity for a groom to show his own style or fashions of the past that are also stylish currently merely because they are old-fashioned. One major faux pas to avoid with the groom's attire is in regards to white tie ensembles (outfits that are all or mostly all white). White tie apparel is only to be used for formal evening weddings and is considered a breach of etiquette to wear one during daytime ceremonies.

Semi-Formal Daytime Attire

Shorter dresses are usually more appropriate attire for the bride for daytime weddings. Any dress length shorter than floor length should be reserved for daytime wedding apparel. This is the scenario where it would be appropriate to wear a short wedding dress either above or below the knee.

If the daytime wedding is not meant to extend into the evening hours, proper etiquette would be to avoid a strapless gown. Semiformal wear for the groom is easily defined as including a short wedding jacket that is usually gray in color and coupled with striped trousers.

Informal Daytime Attire

If you want the most flexibility in terms of wedding attire etiquette, you will want to choose to have an informal ceremony during the daytime before 6 pm. This is when you have the most choices regarding attire while still adhering to wedding etiquette guidelines.

Appropriate bridal wear can be just about anything the bride chooses – within reason, of course. The main etiquette guideline for the bride to remember when choosing her ensemble for an informal daytime wedding is the need to choose something that fits well with the style and theme of the wedding overall.

It is not appropriate for the bride to be grossly overdressed in comparison to the rest of the wedding party at an informal ceremony. The wedding dress can be long or short with a variety of fabrics and styles. This is the most appropriate time for a wedding dress that has colored accents other than white or ivory, and perfectly appropriate to match colors in the wedding dress to colors in the groom's floral or artistic tie complementing a light summer suit.

Informal Evening Attire

The etiquette involved with an informal evening wedding gives a nice mixture of possibilities with nothing too extreme. In terms of a strapless wedding gown, a wedding in the evening is the appropriate place for such a dress but when it is also informal, it is perfectly appropriate to be a shorter wedding dress along with being strapless. The groom can wear a less formal black suit instead of a tux, with a "quieter" tie instead of the traditional ties necessary with formal evening wedding attire.

Attendant Attire Etiquette

Bridesmaids Attire

Traditional etiquette for bridesmaids' dresses used to dictate they all wear the same dress in the same color differing only by size. Anyone who has been a bridesmaid either carries "horror" stories of the awful dress the bride asked them to wear that was personally unflattering to their particular body dynamics (such as asking a bridesmaid with a body flaw of flabby, overweight arms being asked to wear the same sleeveless dress everyone else was wearing, etc.), or is afraid of what the bride is going to ask them to wear.

Etiquette rules in this area have loosened considerably allowing the bride to offer some great options to those she would like to be a part of her bridal party.

Different Dress Options – These options can allow a happy compromise for all by giving the bride the details most important to her while also respecting the individual needs of her bridesmaids. The choices can be allowed by style, color, and/or neckline.

- **By Style** – You may offer your bridesmaids the option of choosing whatever style of dress they prefer as long as the color and shade is the exactly the same. Many designers creating bridesmaids dresses currently will often offer a variety of styles for whatever your specific color choice is for the bridesmaids' dresses.

- **By Specific Color** – You can give the option of a range of specific color choices that complement your wedding fantasies. For example, you have chosen to have a formal evening wedding with the main colors of deep purple and black. You could ask your bridesmaids to wear strapless, floor length gowns either purple or black.

- **By Color Hue** – A trend in bridesmaids' dresses that is becoming more popular is allowing the bridesmaids to choose what shade of a specific color you would like them to wear in specific styles, and/or also allowing them to choose the style along with the color shade. Choosing their own shade of color allows them to choose what shade they believe best compliments their own skin tones. Allowing the girls their choice in color shade and style just may cause your bridesmaids to consider you their most favorite bride ever as any body areas they are uncomfortable with can be handled in ways that allow them to actually enjoy being a part of your wedding party instead of dreading it self-consciously.

- **Caution** – It would be wise to specifically state dress choices that would not be acceptable for your wedding because of personal preference, location, or etiquette. Don't just assume your bridesmaids all know what would be considered appropriate etiquette or not because you may just get a shock on your wedding day when one of your bridesmaids shows up for your conservative church wedding in an outfit that is the perfect color, but looks like something a stripper would wear on a street corner!

Matching Bridesmaids Dresses – If you prefer your bridesmaids all wear the same dress, wedding etiquette suggests you carefully choose a dress silhouette that will complement the bodies of most or all the women in your wedding.

While traditional etiquette used to disallow strapless or short dresses for the bridesmaids, they are considered appropriate for today's trends. Black bridesmaids' dresses used to also be taboo in wedding etiquette but are fast becoming an acceptable trend to which many bridesmaids respond with great appreciation.

When deciding on bridesmaids' dresses, there are a few things to consider from an etiquette concern centered on the welfare and happiness of your bridesmaids.

- **Comfort** – Try to choose a dress that will allow your attendants to be comfortable wearing for many hours that will also allow them to fully participate in any wedding activities easily such as dancing at the reception. Equally important are the shoes you ask them to wear. It is rude to ask the people to wear painful, uncomfortable shoes for the sake of appearance. Remember they will be wearing the shoes for long hours just as you will and miserable feet sure will cut down on pleasure and enjoyment of the wedding festivities!

- **Usability** – It is not only kind, but also appropriate etiquette to at least consider the bridesmaids' dresses you are requesting to be such that can be worn for other occasions after your wedding is over. Today's economy has most people on a tight budget which includes your bridesmaids who may struggle to afford to buy the dress wedding etiquette dictates they pay for themselves in most cases so it is impolite to ask them to buy a dress that they will never be able to wear again because of its color, style, or formality. Having this detail high on your priority list will give the women another reason to be happy as a part of your wedding party.

- **Length** – Old-fashioned wedding etiquette used to be that the length of the bridesmaids' dresses was dependent on the type of wedding similar to the etiquette defining the bride's wedding dress such as strapless only in evening weddings, floor-length a must for formal weddings, etc. These days the only important etiquette for this point is that the bridesmaids' dresses complement the formality and style of wedding they will be standing in – much like the bridal guidelines for informal daytime weddings. A short, casual dress would be out of place for a formal evening wedding just as a floor length satin dress would not fit right in a ceremony held outdoors during the daytime. Common sense is the main etiquette dictate for this aspect of your wedding.

Groomsmen Attire

The clothing for the groomsmen may well be the easiest part of your wedding to plan as the choices are limited, but the etiquette details involved may well cost the groomsmen more financially than what bridesmaids may be paying for their outfits.

But there are etiquette suggestions that will be affordable for your groomsmen without causing glaring problems in the overall wedding style portrayed.

- **Suits & Tuxedos** – It is usually easiest and least expensive for your groomsmen to rent their apparel for the wedding as that most often includes the accessories such as shoes, etc. that need to be appropriate for the occasion. This is also the easiest way to coordinate their attire with the bridesmaids' dresses since color coordinating is rarely a favorite activity for the average man.

Renting their attire is considerably easier for most and definitely cheaper since it includes everything including the colored ties, cummerbunds, etc., that most of them will not already own. When the men are asked to wear their own suits and other articles, they will usually wind up having to buy more accessories than the girls will, as they will need dressy shoes that match, belts, etc.

If you are asking them to wear their own clothing, simple requests such as the color of the shoes or belt buckle are appropriate without expecting them to buy expensive accessories that they may not already own nor will have much use for after the wedding. You can ask all the men to wear black leather shoes, silver belt buckles, etc., which are all appropriate requests of the ones asked to be a part of your ceremony.

- **Color** – The most common and popular choice for groomsmen apparel is a black tuxedo which is appropriate unless your ceremony is on a beach during the day. And if your groomsmen already own a tux, most often they will have a black tux in their closet to use for such formal occasions and will only need to follow your preferences in the color and style of accessories.

- **Formal Attire** – When white tie formal wear is requested, the etiquette guidelines are simple but limiting. It usually means wearing a black tailcoat with matching pants along with a stiff, white shirt with a white bow tie and vest and optional white or gray gloves along with black shoes and socks.

If your wedding is to be a black tie event, groomsmen should wear a black tuxedo again with matching paints, a formal white shirt, with matching bow tie and cummerbund or vest along with black shoes and socks. Summer etiquette rules allow for a white dinner jacket along with black pants and a black tie for more informal weddings.

- **Ultimate Casual** – When you are having an informal and casual daytime wedding, it is appropriate etiquette for groomsmen to wear khaki pants with casual button down shirts or even khaki shorts with polo shirts if it will fit with the overall casual style of your wedding.

Wedding Guest Attire

There are certain etiquette protocols that are should be universally followed by wedding guests without reminder or emphasis, and there are attire options and etiquette that are perfectly acceptable for you to request in the wedding invitation. Most guests greatly appreciate when an invitation includes attire suggestions that help make the wedding more meaningful to you.

- **White Tie** – If white tie formal wear is requested, male guests should wear a tailcoat with a stiff white shirt, vest, and tie along with white or gray gloves and black shoes. Ladies need to wear formal, floor-length gowns in any color but white (in order to not upstage the traditional white bridal gown).

- **Black Tie** – For a black tie wedding, men should wear a black tux or evening jacket with matching pants but no white tie. Black ties, vests, or cummerbunds are fine. For summer weddings, a white dinner jacket with black pants is appropriate. Ladies can go black tie with dressier, floor length gowns, or shorter, but dressy cocktail style dresses.

- **Optional Black Tie** – When a wedding invitation states "black tie optional", etiquette to follow allows guests to wear the same outfits black tie events require, or they can go a little more casual which for men translates to a dark suit with a tie that blends in without making a statement. Tuxedos are considered the optional part of this scenario. Ladies can wear the same black tie outfits or it is perfectly appropriate to choose more casual gowns and even dressy separates if desired.

- **Semi-Formal** – Semi-formal wear requested means men can wear a dark suit with a white shirt and understated tie, and women can wear cocktail style dresses, or long skirts with a top (both separates classified as dressy). When the wedding invitation is not specific concerning attire, wedding etiquette guidelines to follow are those for semi-formal ensembles.

- **Casual Attire** – Dressing for a casual wedding usually depends on where the wedding being held. It is appropriate for male guests to wear button down shirts with a tie and khaki pants or even shorts for an outdoor wedding while female guests find a sundress the perfect choice for the same wedding. The etiquette detail to be most aware of when attending a casual wedding is making sure your clothing is not too formal for the situation.

Parents of the Bride and Groom Apparel

Mothers – There are some unique rules of etiquette that the mother of the bride and the mother of the groom need to follow when it comes to their dress choices for the wedding day. The guidelines are rather simple, but very important to follow if concerned with proper etiquette.

The main thing to remember is the mother of the bride is to choose her dress first and then inform the mother of the groom what her choice of dress is. The mother of the groom then needs to choose a dress that will compliment but not necessarily match the dress the bride's mother is wearing with the emphasis being on not clashing rather than trying to match colors.

The only other thing to remember is the length of the dresses chosen by the mothers is dictated by the style of the wedding along with the length of the bridesmaids' dresses.

Fathers – The etiquette for the fathers of the bride and groom to follow in terms of wedding attire are most likely the simplest guidelines of the entire wedding. The fathers' choices in clothing should reflect the formality in style chosen for the wedding ceremony and will most often be the most formally dressed group in any wedding.

When formal suits or tuxedoes are appropriate, it is acceptable in terms of etiquette to ask that the formal accessories be chosen to match the colors of the bridesmaids' dresses or they can also rent the same style of tuxedos the groomsmen will be wearing.

Chapter 6: Ceremony Etiquette

When it comes to the actual wedding ceremony, some details take a little more consideration than usual in order to create the meaningful ceremony you want without purposefully offending others in a way that will detract from your own enjoyment and memories of the wedding.

Religious Differences

When religious aspects will be an important part of your wedding ceremony, planning can be a little tricky with various levels of importance depending on which religions are involved and whose religion requires a greater degree of respect shown. You will never be able to please everyone completely when different religions are involved but the main goal should be finding the balance between avoiding offending others while also allowing yourself the wedding ceremony that means the most to you.

A wedding is not the place for any kind of religious protest or statement. All that is needed from all sides is the willingness to respect each other's religious without being obviously resistant or purposefully offensive. No one is forced to attend or stand in a wedding – thankfully shotgun weddings and arranged marriages are a thing of the past, at least in America. If your family or friends are unable to respect differences without making a scene by being visibly offended with any aspect, then they need not attend your wedding. It truly is as simple as that.

There are a few suggestions in terms of etiquette that might make things less stressful on your wedding day if you plan appropriately.

From the Bride & Groom's Perspective

Your wedding is exactly that…yours! And while you should attempt to avoid purposefully offending anyone unnecessarily, you should not leave out religious rituals or details that are meaningful to your special day simply because they might be offensive. You are only responsible for working out the differences you might have between your own faiths if they are not the same.

While lower on the priority list but still a necessary priority, you should also be willing to compromise over differences with anyone who is paying for significant portions of the wedding such as your parents.

If you do not want to attempt to compromise with your parents, then do not allow them to pay for your ceremony. But on the flipside, it is usually inappropriate for the parents to demand religious details be adhered to in order for them to be willing to pay.

From the Perspectives of Everyone Else

Weddings are never a place for religious posturing, protesting, or proselytizing…from any direction. Guests should not be expected to participate in religious aspects of the wedding ceremony if it is against their beliefs to do so.

For example, you should never ask an atheist to offer or read a prayer during your ceremony, but it is appropriate to expect common courtesy and respect from an atheist when others are praying. It is good etiquette for any guest to simply "be" while something is going on in the religious realm that they do not agree with realizing that lack of protest does not mean they agree with the practice or religious element.

It is polite for the guests to stand if others are standing and that does not indicate agreement or participation but merely offers appropriate respect. Essentially, guests need to just "go along" with whatever is occurring within a ceremony but only to the degree that they are comfortable with that will not force them to do anything that offends their own beliefs. Standing with others who are standing may be comfortable for some while kneeling with others kneeling may not be so comfortable.

When guests are attending a wedding that is contrary to their own beliefs, the priority should be respect your religion(s) while not disrespecting their own religion or going against their own beliefs. If that cannot be done in a dignified manner, then those guests should not attend and you might consider not even sending an invitation if you believe there is a good chance they might make a scene at your wedding because of religious differences.

Vows

Whether writing your own vows or following traditional wedding vows, it is important to remember the vows are actually promises you are making to each other and your own personal preferences and beliefs should take priority with any vows you make.

The etiquette involved with the actual wedding vows in a ceremony is much more flexible than probably any other single aspect of your wedding because the vows must be honest and genuine without promising to do something you are not willing to agree to simply because it is expected.

When you write your own vows, you can make sure all wording is exactly what you have agreed on beforehand. Using traditional vows may be preferred either because they are required within whatever religion is relevant to you, or because you want to enjoy the traditional vows that your ancestors used. In most cases, even traditional vows can be tweaked a little to make them acceptable to your own beliefs.

For example, traditional vows used most frequently call for the bride to agree to "obey" the man she is marrying. This is becoming more and more unacceptable with many brides unwilling to agree to such a disrespectful and misogynistic principle. But that particular etiquette problem can be easily solved simply by dropping the word "obey" and anything else that supports that idea while still using the rest of the traditional vows that brides and grooms have spoken for decades.

If you want to write your own vows, or revise popular and traditional vows to express your own styles and personalities, a few things need to be considered in order for your vows to follow some loose etiquette standards.

- You should decide on the principles of your vows together as you are the ones making promises to each other. You need to agree with the vows to each other, or not even make them at all. If you cannot come to a place of agreement just in your vows, then your lives will probably not mix well either and you might want to consider postponing the wedding at that point. With the popularity of writing your own vows on the rise in today's society, so is the desire to "surprise" your spouse by keeping the vows secret until they are needed in the actual wedding ceremony. In terms of etiquette, this might not be such a good idea but if you insist on surprising your spouse with the vows you are willing to make, you should at least agree on the outline and general principles the vows are expected to portray.

- It is also important to check with the minister or church where you are planning to have a religious and/or cultural ceremony since some religions require certain wording or rituals. Even when your religion requires specific vows to be made, there should be an allowance of revision to the expected vows in any area that is a place of disagreement such as the "obey" wording mentioned above.

- In a nutshell, the etiquette rules for wedding vows should not force either bride or groom to vow to do anything or not do anything they are unwilling or uncomfortable with promising and keeping throughout the marriage.

Walking Down the Aisle

As with many traditional etiquette rules in terms of wedding planning and ceremonies, the old guidelines for walking down the aisle have become more relaxed allowing a wedding procession to become more personalized for unique situations and preferences. But there are some similarities in etiquette that are either still kept, expected to be kept, or helpful to know in general in order to change it in ways that are important to you.

Attendants

The walk down the aisle or set placement of the attendants has many variations, but general guidelines are for the groom and groomsmen to be waiting at the altar when the ceremony begins. Then the bridesmaids will walk down the aisle one by one alone with the maid of honor walking last.

If your wedding party is large, it is acceptable for the bridesmaids to be paired with their corresponding groomsman while walking down the aisle at the start of the ceremony instead of just at the end which is more commonly done. They are followed by the flower girl and ring bearer walking down together while the flower girl scatters flower petals along the aisle as she walks down it.

Bride

The bride walks down the aisle after the flower girl and ring bearer and is traditionally accompanied by her father. When family dynamics or death makes this either impossible or unacceptable to the bride, she can walk down the aisle alone, or choose someone else other than her father to walk with her.

It has become acceptable etiquette for the bride's mother to walk the bride down the aisle as well, with or without the father if preferred. Etiquette also suggestions the bride walks down the aisle to the left of whoever is accompanying her.

Attendant Choices

Choosing your attendants can be one of the most enjoyable aspects of planning your wedding but can also be one of the most stressful parts since you usually do not have enough room for all of your close friends, family, and potential in-laws. It might be a little tricky to make these decisions without offending anyone, but ultimately, it is your day and your choice as to who you want as attendants.

The process of choosing will become easier if you prioritize what is important to you and make decisions based on those priorities.

Number

Etiquette for how many bridesmaids and groomsmen you have in your wedding is generally stated as one bridesmaid/groomsman pair for every 50 guests but that is somewhat flexible. You may prefer fewer or more attendants usually depending on how many are on your "short list" for possible attendants.

However, a small wedding should never have more than 12 pairs of attendants and keep in mind the fewer ratios you have in terms of attendants to guests the less appropriate the whole style of your wedding may seem. You do not want to have 12 attendant pairs if you want your wedding to be small and intimate and you are expecting less than 50 people. That would look rather foolish and exhibit an embarrassing breach of wedding etiquette.

Specific People

Most common wedding etiquette suggests that your blood sisters and brothers should be a part of the wedding party. The maid of honor is most often one of the bride's sisters, and the best man is usually the brother or even the father of the groom. It is appropriate to include blood sisters of the groom as bridesmaids and blood brothers of the bride as groomsmen which have the added benefit of strengthening relationships between the families.

Circumstances

When choosing your attendants, make a list of those who are most special in your lives, then begin to narrow the list according to a few aspects from an etiquette perspective.

- Can they financially afford the money it usually costs to be an attendant such as dress, travel, loss of work? If money is the only obstacle can you afford (without resentment) to make up the difference?

- Will they be able to meet the common responsibilities of an attendant such as the bridal shower, bachelor party, helping with the bridal gown selection, addressing the invitation etc.?

- Are they physically capable of being an attendant in your wedding with health limitations that can or cannot be accommodated?

- Will they be an asset to the wedding plans and ceremony as a low-maintenance attendant able to problem solve and be helpful in diffusing conflict if necessary without creating or adding to it?

- Would agreeing to be one of your attendants place an undue burden with their current life circumstances such as location, career, new baby, new spouse, family illness, etc.?

- Are their choices to make that will be more valuable in terms of creating bonds between the two families?

Choosing your attendants is an important part of your wedding plans, and following proper etiquette in doing so is important.

Open communication is vital when determining your attendants and you must be willing to accept a "no" response to your request without getting offended.

If someone does tell you "no" and the reasons why are not obvious, think about it a little while and then ask them why in order to find out if they truly do want to be a part but are struggling with some obstacle or another that might be easily resolved.

It is completely appropriate for anyone to respectfully decline your attendant invitation, and it is appropriate for you to respectfully refrain from asking anyone to attend you whether expected or not. It is inappropriate etiquette for either scenario to result in the total collapse of an important relationship.

But remember, ultimately it is your day so choose attendants according to who will be the most meaningful choices to you and the harmony of your future family life together.

Chapter 7: Wedding Exit Etiquette

Your formal departure from the wedding and reception symbolizes the start of your life together and is usually a highlight to any wedding both from your own perspective as well as from the perspective of family and friends in attendance. Traditional etiquette sets the following pattern:

Bouquet Toss

The bridal ritual of tossing her bouquet of flowers over her shoulder to the single women (guest and attendants both) waiting behind her begins the leave-taking process. This is a fun tradition with the mythical belief that whoever catches the bouquet will be the next one to get married.

Change of Formal Clothing

After the bouquet toss, most often you will then change into "going away" outfits. Usually the outfits are similar in style to what might be worn to an informal evening wedding. You may change separately with your attendants' help and quite often receive last minute advice and well wishes from respective mother or father before meeting up to return to wherever the guests are congregated.

Send Off

The traditional wedding send off of the happy couple consists of running down a path toward the "get away" car while everyone showers you with uncooked white rice that was given to them in an elegant sachet created specifically for that purpose and either placed at their table settings during the reception dinner, or handed out while waiting for you to reappear after changing into your going away outfits.

Recent trends of throwing rice have shifted somewhat because scientific discoveries seem to indicate white rice is harmful to the birds who will eat it off the ground after everyone has left the location. Because of that, many weddings will use birdseed in their send off sachets instead of the traditional rice when they prefer the more traditional send offs.

It has also become popular and perhaps more enjoyable for you to be sent off through a rain of bubbles being blown by the guests surrounding the walkway, and many wedding supply sources offer tiny bottles of decorative bubbles that match the wedding style. Using bubbles at this time also creates some unique and impressive pictures from a photography standpoint as camera lights flash off the bubbles and create uniquely beautiful pictures.

Bubbles are also a great choice in terms of clean up not only of the grounds, but also for the people who have either been targeted, or have simply gotten in the way of enthusiastic guests. Butterflies, silly string, flower petals, doves, confetti, or champagne poppers are all acceptable alternatives to rice and the costs vary accordingly.

Getaway Car

The getaway car and how it is decorated (or not) can give an exciting and memorable ending to the wedding as well as a fun beginning to life together as a new couple, or it end the wedding on a sour note depending on the circumstances that are unique to your own preferences and taste.

While you should have a good sense of humor, this is an area that people frequently and willfully ignore proper manners and etiquette so you will do well to determine in advance just how willing you are to tolerate pranks with your getaway car.

Complete Avoidance of Car Decorating

If you do not want your car decorated at all, you can take a few precautions that might help you avoid it. For example, you can keep it a secret where your car is parked, be vague about which car you will be driving to get away, use cabs or limos for the getaway, or literally hire guards or assign family to make sure your car is not trashed.

Self-Decorated

It is appropriate to decorate your getaway car yourselves and include the details that will make it most enjoyable for you (i.e. with or without cans tied to the back, with or without writing on the back windshield, with or without balloons, etc.) Decorating it yourself or designating trusted loved ones to do so might help you avoid (if wanted) the shenanigans of known pranksters in your group when they see it has already been done.

Partially Decorated

You may want to allow some decorating of the getaway car as a fun tradition to follow and enjoy with your more whimsical and mischievous friends. An easy way to limit the decorations is by making sure the doors are locked with the keys secured so that only the outside of the car is decorated.

You can also create a situation where the car is only available for decoration just a few short minutes before you leave which won't leave enough time for some of the more obnoxious pranks. You can also sure there is someone possessing common sense monitoring the decorations in order to keep anyone from going overboard.

Free-For-All

Of course you have the freedom of just letting go and whatever happens to your car, happens, but remember, some people take complete leave of their senses when it comes to pranks and decorating getaways cars at weddings. This is the time when etiquette guidelines tend to get easily ignored and crazy things become part of the end of your wedding day that may not be acceptable to either of you.

Some of the unacceptable pranks void of etiquette and manners might include decorating the car with personal hygiene or sexually oriented items, filling the interior of the car with packing peanuts, wrapping the entire car with plastic wrap, gluing the doors closed forcing bride and groom to crawl through the windows, etc.

Getaway Car Don'ts & Do's

Guests should be led by example when it comes to taking the initiative for decorating a getaway car. They should follow the examples set by family members on both sides and if no one is even thinking about decorating the car, then accept their wisdom and trust that you may want no part in a decorated getaway car whatsoever.

Etiquette rules give the following guidelines for DO NOT DO when decorating a getaway car:

- NO personal hygiene or intimate products should ever be used to decorate a car. That is considered trashy and distasteful with some particular choices being highly offensive to conservative members of the family, bridal party, or even locations such as a church. These items are simply not appropriate or in good taste for any send off.

- Toilet paper should not be used either. It is messy to clean up, not environmentally friendly and considered crude by most etiquette standards.

- Shaving cream and liquid shoe polish are not good choices either as they can easily do permanent damage to the car's paint job and interior if accidentally transferred inside during the bedlam.

Car friendly liquid chalk or window markers are usually a good choice for expressing the appropriate sentiments on the car windows. Just be careful not to limit the driver's vision field as there would be no worse time for a car accident than when you officially head off into the sunset of your life together.

- Silly string, confetti, glitter, and powder are all less than desirable while decorating a car or for throwing while you are getting into your car. These all are very hard to clean up either before you depart on your wedding trip via the airport or when you return home to the mess that was your car. While it may be considered in good fun to shower them with such things, it is more so considered a serious breach of etiquette, and really quite rude unless that is something you specifically ask for at send-off.

- Delayed entry pranks are also frowned on from a proper etiquette viewpoint and can be upsetting to one or both of you during a time you should just be enjoying the memories that are being made. These types of unacceptable pranks would include anything that causes you to struggle to get into your car with things that take longer than a couple of seconds to navigate. For example, putting a few balloons inside the car is acceptable etiquette, but stuffing the entire car as full of balloons as possible requiring significant time in removing balloons before you can leave is not acceptable. Wrapping a car with one layer of plastic wrap might be tolerated and easily removed, but wrapping up the car like a package being drop-shipped is not considered good etiquette.

Beloved traditions and appropriate etiquette of things TO DO when decorating a getaway car:

- Think ahead of special touches that would be particularly enjoyable, meaningful, and memorable for yourselves or for others to give you. Things like a magnetic sign that gives the date and "Just Married" that can be reused every year on your anniversary, etc., an angel or other significant religious symbol on the front grill of the car, signs or symbols that are special to you such as military symbols, career-related symbols, or things related to your intended future.

- Use ribbon or netting while decorating to ensure the car is not scratched or damaged by the decorations.

- Tell your wedding party or loved ones beforehand if you would be disappointed by not having the traditional tin cans, plastic bottles, and old shoes as noisemakers tied to the bumper of your car like as been traditional for a noisy send off for decades. It is a cute tradition that is inexpensive, environmental-friendly, and considered by most to be just good, old-fashioned fun.

- Vinyl window clings are also a thoughtful way to decorate the getaway car that can eventually be removed or rearranged or left on to enjoy for as long as you want to.

- Craft and wedding supply stores will usually carry car-decorating kits that are sure to be safe and non-toxic for the car and the people involved. This might be the easiest way to decorate the car whether you are doing so yourself for your own wedding, or if you want to delegate the car decorating task to others.

Conclusion

When disagreements and conflicts begin to pop up as they inevitably will while planning and executing a "dream" wedding, future happiness, and cooperation between the two families being joined together needs to have the highest priority.

The wedding day is not what is going to make or break your lives together, but it could very well place some pretty difficult obstacles in your future if you are not conscious of some of the important etiquette guidelines that surround this momentous occasion!

As long as you do not carry an intention to offend or hurt loved ones or remain ignorant of wedding etiquette for whatever reason, you will be able to enjoy your wedding day with a clear conscience with all the unique personalization that will make it the most special and memorable for years to come.

Made in the USA
Middletown, DE
03 February 2017